Breaking Broke

*Destroying the mindset and habits
that keep you broke*

By Angela Ellis

ANGELA ELLIS

Cover design by O. O. Esther
Interior design by Panagiotis Lampridis
Photography by Gregg E. Johnson
Manufactured in the United States of America

ISBN 9781676783077

DEDICATION

I dedicate **Breaking Broke** *to my mother, Claretta Hills Ellis. Mama, you are my inspiration, my number one fan, and my constant source of encouragement. You recently reminded me that you always knew I would be financially savvy because as a young girl I asked for a savings account. Then I demanded to speak to the bank manager to have service fees refunded. That was my first financial success story which you made possible by supporting me.*

Thank you for encouraging me in my journey to authorship which started in the early years. Thank you for helping me get my poetry copyrighted and published as a teen.

You have worried for me, leaving no need for me to worry. You have celebrated me even when I didn't think to celebrate myself. When I was growing up, you and Daddy gave me the freedom to try new things and take risks. How amazing it was to grow up believing that life was limitless. And, still in my adulthood, you have continued to express pride and joy in me that has boosted me and reminded me that anything is possible.

In Loving Memory of my father, Robert Ellis Sr.

September 13, 1936 – March 5, 2010

Daddy, I miss you every day.

ACKNOWLEDGMENTS

Thanks to my many mentors
for encouraging my development.

Thanks to my coach for helping me
find the right paths.

Thanks to my partner who is my
sounding board and advocate.

Thanks to all my friends and family who have
supported me in this journey.

Table of Contents

INTRODUCTION

I was a twenty-five-year-old college graduate. I had recently moved to a new city 600 miles away from my entire family. And I was $100,000 in debt. It was debt which I accumulated through a series of bad choices. Although I had a lot of fun creating that debt, I knew it had to go. Before I was twenty-eight years old, I had eliminated all of it, bought a home, and saved a comfortable nest egg, too.

Later in life disaster struck. With imminent health, employment, and relationship issues, I once again had debt exceeding six figures. This time I knew what to do. Within less than two years I had eradicated all the debt and have remained debt free.

I didn't receive an inheritance. I didn't win the lottery. However, I did embark on an unforgettable journey during which I learned a lot about myself. I learned from my own mistakes and the devastating errors I saw others making. I also discovered that being broke is not just a state of finances; it is a state of **mind**.

ANGELA ELLIS

Where and how you grow up shapes how you think about money. Your habits and values inform your financial choices. Everyone's relationship with money determines how **broke** they are and how ***broken*** they remain. *I share my story so others can learn in a few days what it took me twenty years to figure out.*

Youthful Indulgence

Many times, people have asked me how I amassed such a huge amount of debt so early in life. I often reply, *"Just lucky I guess."* When I first stepped onto a college campus, it was glorious. The rolling hills and beautiful landscapes were peppered with laughter, music, and conversation. Those hills were also sprinkled with creditors looking to give credit cards to unsuspecting teenagers. I was seventeen years old when I stepped onto that campus, and before taking my first class, I had applied for and received my first credit card. By the end of my undergraduate career, I had collected eleven credit cards, all of which were maxed out. This was the beginning of my indebtedness.

Despite a few scholarships and grants, I had also accumulated some student loan debt—all of which I was taking with me as I started my new life in the "real world." At age twenty-two I moved to a different city and started a new life that came with a hefty price tag. I bought lots of new furniture for my new apartment, bought a brand-new car, and purchased several appliances. I took a Caribbean girls' trip once a year also. All these things were paid for on credit. At the time when I decided the debt must go, I was earning about $27,000 a year. I had no savings and no financial gurus in my life to guide me. But I knew something had to change. I had seen all those famous financial experts on television sharing tips for reducing debt, improving credit, and stabilizing spending. I started doing some research and planning my strategy.

MINDSET CYCLES

Mindset Cycles

While I was in college, I had a roommate I'll call Elle. In high school, math wasn't Elle's favorite subject. In fact, it was her least favorite subject. Her parents hired tutors for her who did the best they could to help her do better as a student. Nevertheless, Elle was convinced she could never be good at math. The more she uttered this thought, the more she gave life to it. She believed it and her grades reflected it. She adopted the attitude that math wasn't her thing and there was no point in trying, so she didn't. She stopped studying and gave her attention to other subjects which she enjoyed more. Once Elle got to college, all of that math avoidance started to catch up with her. She was ill-prepared for advanced mathematics such as trigonometry and calculus.

She found that her decisions, actions, and circumstances had been greatly impacted by her thoughts, beliefs, and attitudes. As her roommate, I became her tutor and study partner. But we could not catch up in one semester what she had been neglecting for four years. It later affected her subsequent career choices. Although she was interested in biotechnology, a career in any area of science or technology would be difficult without strong math skills.

I learned from Elle, that today's decisions rarely impact today alone. Unfortunately, I didn't think about that when I was making all those purchases during college and thereafter.

Your decisions from five years ago impact today. Financial decisions from today will still impact you and your family five years from now. Every purchasing decision that creates debt can be long lasting and upset opportunities later on. What I learned from Elle and myself was that decisions— especially financial ones—are lasting and impactful. I realized that changing my spending habits wouldn't be enough. I had to change my mindset and my relationship with money. I had to leverage its power, rather than giving money power. I had to take back control.

Meet T.O.D.
Talent, Opportunity, and Drive

The first part of breaking a broke mindset is finding the motivation to mobilize yourself. A wise man once stated:

"The universe distributes equal amounts of talent to everyone, but unequal amounts of opportunity and drive."

You probably know someone who is gifted and smart but doesn't have the drive or motivation to leverage their giftedness. You may even know someone who is talented in many ways but lives in such a depressed environment, family, or situation, they don't have opportunities to explore their talents to the fullest.

One example of this is Donnie. He seemed to have been born with an abundance of raw talents in lots of areas. He could play musical instruments and even taught himself to read and write music. He was an awarded athlete and he also performed well in school. Yet he had no drive. He didn't want to do anything with any of those God-given skills. He was offered college scholarships and turned them down because he didn't want to leave the comfort and familiarity of his parents' home. He had good paying jobs but always managed to lose them because he showed up late, goofed off at work, or didn't show up at all.

Donnie met and fell in love with a nice girl who wanted to move him to the West Coast to work at her dad's business. She booked a flight for him and made all the arrangements. Donnie didn't show up for that flight, and shortly thereafter he broke it off with that girl. You see, Donnie had talents and had been presented with many opportunities, but he never had the drive to do anything meaningful with his life. Despite their best efforts, friends and family couldn't help Donnie. Only Donnie could help Donnie, and he wouldn't.

When you don't have the drive to do things differently, you just won't. You may have the talent, you may even have the opportunity, but a lack of drive will always keep you stuck. Science teaches us that things that are in motion tend to stay in motion, and things that are immobile tend to stay immobile. Donnie was motionless and determined to stay there. Perhaps he had a mindset of fear or complacency that prevented him from moving forward.

When I decided to change my financial condition, I examined my thoughts and beliefs. I had to *believe* I could do it before I could be motivated to take action. If you have bought the financial books, listened to the podcasts, and attended the classes but your finances haven't drastically changed, you may not be exercising your T.O.D. You may already know the right moves to make, but you haven't made them. Why haven't you?

Why haven't you taken those steps that you know you should, that you know will work, that you know could change your situation or even your entire life? It could be a lack of motivation. You need to know that the changes will be worth it. You need to fully believe the changes you make will work out in your favor. In order to get unstuck you must believe in the dream—you need to believe it can become reality. Also, you must believe the dream is worth your time, effort, and even worth the risk.

Start by writing down a list of dreams you have for yourself, your family, and your future. Do you want to own a home? Do you want to be debt free? Do you want to start a scholarship fund for wounded warriors? Do you want to buy your next car with cash? Whatever that dream is, write it down. Be detailed in your descriptions. It might look something like this:

"I want to have enough money saved to go to Hawaii with my wife and son in the next five years. I want to be able to pay for the entire trip with cash."

Once you see it on paper you can visualize it in your mind. Then, you can start to believe it and take steps to make it a reality.

Commitment and Consistency

Achieving your goal will take commitment and consistency, which is the second part to breaking a broke mindset. You'll have to examine the little things you do every day.

Our troubles and our triumphs start with our choices.

Whether you want to become a millionaire, save for your children's college, or pay off your debt, you have to understand that there is no magic pill or potion. You will have to do the work. If your journey is anything like mine, it will be a process of learning, discovery, adjustment, and reward. So, get ready!

The One Month Challenge

You can start by writing down everything you spend for thirty days. At the end of each day, think back to what you have purchased, loaned to others, given away, or gambled away. This does not include your monthly bills. Those are your primary expenses and they are not optional. Your list will consist of other secondary purchases you make over the course of a month. Account for every pack of gum, every soda, and write down how much it cost.

When I did this, I used a notetaking app on my phone to track each expenditure immediately. At the end of the month I circled all the things I spent money on that were *necessities*: groceries, medication, school supplies, a doctor's visit, and vehicle service. Then I totaled up all the money I spent on things that were *not* necessities. How do you know if it's a necessity? Ask yourself if you could have survived and been healthy and safe without that purchase. If not, it is a necessity. You need your medication to be healthy. Your car needs good tires to be safe. You need to buy groceries for your family for nourishment and survival. All those things are necessary items for basic life needs.

Here's what your list might look like at the end of the month. In fact, it could look like this in just one week:

Packs of gum	$5
Coffee at coffee shop	$5
Prescription meds	$20
Lipstick	$16
Hair appointment	$90
Throw pillows for sofa	$50
Allergy medicine	$25
New dress	$59
New cell phone case	$30
Concert tickets	$120
T-shirt at concert	$25
Birthday gift for neighbor	$30
Sunscreen	$9
Toilet tissue	$10

Fruit	$30
School uniforms	$100

In the above example, there was more than $450 spent on non-necessities. The lipstick, new dress, throw pillows, phone case, and concert tickets were among the non-essentials. Your last step is to determine how you could have spent that money in ways that might have a more positive, long-term impact for you or your family. Make sure you make a written list.

For example:

Pay extra on credit card bill	$200
Pay off remaining furniture bill in full	$200
Take grandkids to the zoo	$50

I'm not suggesting that you will never spend money on non-essentials. I'm not even suggesting that spending money on non-essentials is bad or wrong. This exercise is simply designed to help you identify areas where your money could be spent more wisely.

Making It Stick

It stands to reason that if you're going to pay down debt, you can't continue to accumulate new debts. There is a mindset it takes to make these choices. If you're not quite there yet, keep contemplating it, thinking about it, talking about it, and praying about it. Remember, the breaking broke mindset suggests that you *think* your way to different behavior.

For all of us, what we think influences what we believe. What we believe influences what we do. And what we do influences our future.

What you think about money drives what you do. What you believe about money drives your money-related behavior. If you believe money is complicated, you will be confused by it. If you believe it is more powerful than you, it will have power over you. If you believe it's elusive, you will let it control you instead of you controlling it. If you believe money is a tool, you will leverage it to **build** something great.

Impressions

You've heard of keeping up with the Joneses. Well, trying to impress the Joneses is just as harmful to your financial state. The right mindset will help you avoid these traps. We, as a society, are socialized to make the right impression. This can sometimes lead to doing things we cannot afford to do and buying things we cannot afford to buy. Symbols of our status—like homes, cars, vacations, and dinner parties—are how our society signals success. If we don't have the trappings that signal our success, then we might not look and feel successful. We're conditioned to want to impress others. In order to break broke, that traditional societal mindset has to change. It is keeping us broke. Write this on a sticky note and place it on your bathroom mirror or dashboard:

I have no one to impress but yourself.

One thing that's helpful in adjusting one's mindset is beginning with the end in mind. Identify your short- and long-term goals. Let those goals *replace* your desire to gain approval from others.

Write your goals down and keep them where you will see them every day. I framed mine and placed them on my nightstand. Every morning and night before brushing my teeth, I would read those goals and reflect on my progress. This technique is a great reminder of why you're making big changes in your spending and lifestyle habits. Your "why" must be bigger than your excuses.

The next time you are tempted to upgrade to a more luxurious car, stop and remember your goals. If you find yourself contemplating a home-equity loan to build a deck to your home, consider your priorities. And remember:

There is nothing impressive about a mountain of debt.

What You Can Afford

Buy only what you can afford. What does that mean? You can truly afford something *only* if you can buy it without going into debt. If you must use financing – like a credit card or any kind of loan -- for a purchase, you can't truly afford it. At least you can't afford it right now. Of course, there are a couple of exceptions: houses and cars. Although, if you're willing to make radical changes, you can start buying cars and homes with cash, like I have.

Here's how to make sure you can afford the things you want.

If your family wants to take a vacation that will cost $5,000, you should start saving $5,000. Once you've accumulated that amount (or more) in your savings account, you are ready to take that trip. That may mean this vacation will happen two, three, or maybe even five years from now. But you can make it happen.

I like to call this *Financing Future Fun.* You will have savings for emergencies and necessities also. This, however, is just for the fun stuff. This kind of saving can feel a lot more rewarding because it gives you something to anticipate. When my family uses this technique, there are a few different ways we acquire the funds we need to finance our fun:

1. We identify places where we already have funds accumulated, like savings accounts, money market accounts, and checking accounts. As long as that money is not already allotted for another purpose – like an emergency fund -- it's fair game to use for our vacation.

2. My partner and I often took seasonal or part-time jobs for the sole purpose of saving for something fun—like a vacation. This would allow us to raise additional funds, rather than trying to stretch our existing incomes to cover the additional expense.

3. We hosted garage sales, in person and online. Additionally, we offered to host garage sales for others. We knew that many of our neighbors often talked about having garage sales and were just too busy to make it happen. Therefore, we offer to sell their items for them during our garage sales. The neighbors would bring their goods to us (with prices marked if desired). Then, while they attended to their normal Saturday chores and errands, we would sell their stuff for them. In return for our time and effort, they would pay us 15% of their proceeds.

4. We would use our T.O.D. (talents, opportunities, and drive) to make money. I am a fairly skilled baker and quilt maker. I would bake cakes and make quilts for others for a price. My partner was a talented woodworker. He would make custom tables and benches to make extra cash. Consider the talents you have and how you might leverage them to make money.

5. Get the kids to chip in. My friend Rhonda takes a family trip with her husband and children each year. While planning the vacation, her family holds a meeting to discuss particulars. During the meeting—which takes place six to twelve months in advance—the family decides where they want to go and how they will pay for it. She helps her children learn the value of money and appreciate its purchasing power. Her teenagers have jobs, and she asks them to save part of their earnings to contribute to their own spending money for the family trip. I learned this from Rhonda and started doing the same thing in my household. If you have teenagers, consider asking them to earn some of their own money for things they want to buy.

6. Lean living helps us accumulate cash. You can live leaner by deferring some purchases to later, spending less on non-necessities, and focusing on basics. We'll explore each of these in the next chapter.

ANGELA ELLIS

LIVING LEAN

Lean Living - Cold Turkey

As previously mentioned, writing down everything you purchased for one month, is a good way to identify needless spending habits. Take this a step further with another month-long challenge. It's called the *Cold Turkey Challenge*. During the Cold Turkey Challenge, I went an entire month without making any non-essential purchases. Of course, I still had to pay my bills and fulfill financial obligations. My basic physiological needs of food, shelter, safety, and health were top priority and therefore non-negotiable. For example, I wouldn't buy junk food instead of fresh vegetables, just because junk food is cheaper. Nevertheless, I didn't buy anything that wasn't a primary expense. I didn't purchase a pack of gum or even a cup of coffee.

Radical change requires radical change. This is where it starts.

I've shared this exercise with friends who were instantly looking for a loophole. They told me that if they did this challenge, they would simply buy twice as much of everything during the prior month. That way, they would have enough to last them through their cold turkey month. They told me they would buy everything they thought they might need in larger quantities. During the cold turkey month, they wouldn't have to go without those things they were accustomed to having. That defeats the purpose of the challenge. If you're going to get a sense for what you can do without, you must go without it.

Don't Deceive Yourself; Challenge Yourself.

Stocking up on all your favorite things – candy bars, beer, music downloads, etc. – is not the intent of this challenge. For this month, and the preceding month, purchase groceries as you normally would, refill your prescriptions as needed, and pay your bills on time.

The purpose of this challenge is also to get accustomed to doing without some unnecessary items. Over the course of the month, you will figure out what those things are. I must admit, there were times during the cold turkey challenge when I was bored and wanted to go see a movie. I didn't always feel like cooking and wanted to dine out at one of my favorite restaurants. But I made it through the entire month without any ancillary purchases. I proved to myself that I could exercise discipline. I also learned I could live without many of the things that I habitually purchased.

After my cold turkey month, I wanted to treat myself. I felt I deserved to reward myself for a job well done. Beware of this temptation. After your cold turkey month is over, you will probably want to do the same. Make sure it is a small treat that doesn't eliminate all of the money you just saved.

Your reward should cost less than 10 percent of what you saved.

During my cold turkey challenge, I saved $500. My reward afterwards cost me less than 10 percent of that. I bought myself a new pair of sandals and an ice cream sundae. Why those two things? I discovered during this experience, that new shoes and dessert were the two things I missed the most. On the other hand, I realized I didn't miss buying coffee from a coffee shop. I didn't miss driving there, standing in a long line, and hoping the barista got my order right. After cold turkey, I continued making coffee for myself at home. That was an expense I was able to permanently eliminate.

Your cold turkey month will help you identify what really matters to you. There will be some things you will miss having and you will realize those things matter. Hopefully, you'll find things you don't miss at all. You might be able to stop spending money on those items all together. The *cold turkey challenge* is an opportunity to push yourself outside your comfort zone, identify what really matters, and find areas for cost saving in one month.

Lean Living - Waiting It Out

I know people who finance almost everything in their lives. I bet you know these people, too. It's a way of life for many Americans. One friend of mine, Arthur, had financed all of his home furnishings. Arthur's sofa was completely worn out, but he was still paying for it because he had taken a loan to buy it. He bought a new sofa and financed that one as well. At that point, Arthur was for two sofas: the new one in his living room as well as the remaining balance on the old sofa which was hauled away. The money Arthur was paying for the old sofa was essentially thrown away because he didn't even have that piece of furniture anymore.

When you pay long, you pay wrong.

The financing of the new sofa created a situation that was just as wasteful. Arthur would end up paying for that sofa over several years and pay twice as much as the original purchase price. Ultimately, the sofa he bought for $1,500 would cost him $3,000 because of a rather high interest rate which was compounding monthly.

Arthur made the same purchasing mistakes with his appliances, clothes, and electronics. I know many people who share Arthur's mindset, which is as long as you can finance it, you can afford it. *That is a broke mindset.* With this buying pattern, you always wind up paying too much, paying too long, and being trapped in a cycle of debt.

When I wanted to replace a twenty-year-old sofa that was falling apart, I bought a barely used one from an estate sale. That sofa had literally been covered in plastic and placed in an unused room for decades. I made that purchase with cash. Later on, I was able to sell that vintage sofa to a consignment shop for more than I had paid for it.

Another issue with financing household items, is many times the items wear out before you are finished paying for them.

Paying for something you no longer have is a no-no.

Arthur's sofa is a good example of this. A better strategy for Arthur and people like him is *Waiting It Out.* Waiting it out means deferring a purchase until you have the money for it, in hand. New furniture, electronics, and clothes are usually not emergency purchases. Instead of acquiring debt for such purchases, you can use the *Financing Future Fun* strategies. These strategies allow you to make or 'find' the money you will need for non-essential purchases.

You won't have it instantly, but you can have it eventually.

Sometimes, it's tempting to buy things that make an impression on others. I know what it's like to want a new 70-inch HDTV to impress the neighbors when they come over for the Super Bowl party. I know what it's like to want a new ball gown to wear to a gala, because I don't want to be seen in last year's dress. Again, there is nothing impressive about a mountain of debt. Instead, I shop around and do some price comparisons for purchases like these. I won't have it instantly, but I can have it eventually with proper planning. It takes time to make smart purchases. It takes time to save up for what you want. The time and effort invested will be worth it.

Living Lean - Giving Instead of Spending

When I mention the word "sacrifice," people sometimes roll their eyes and sigh. No one wants to do it or accept that it's necessary. However, if you're in a place where you have five- or six-figure debt, like I had, sacrifice will be necessary. Or, if you have a lofty financial goal and are not quite sure how to reach it, sacrifice will be necessary. You will need to do some things differently if you want to see different results. Spending less is an important and necessary means of breaking old, unproductive habits and changing your financial situation.

One element of spending less is the *80-10-10 rule*. The 80-10-10 rule suggests that a household should be living off of 80 percent of its take-home income. Additionally, a household should be saving 10 percent of its take-home income. Giving or donating the remaining 10 percent is the ultimate goal. Imagine you have $100. Before doing anything else, you would put $10 of that $100 into a savings account of some kind. Then you find a cause or charity you care about and donate $10. You can spend the remaining $80 on your life and lifestyle.

If you're not in the habit of setting aside 10 percent of your income for charitable giving, let me explain this important concept. For people of faith, this is probably a familiar practice. If you are not a person with a religious background, this principle might be new to you. In any case, there are several universal principles that suggest charity is beneficial for prosperity.

What Goes Around Comes Around

Basically, the things that you put out into the world are the things that you attract to you. When you put out generosity, that is what you tend to get back. When you exude selfishness, nothing comes back except selfishness. When your hands are open to give, they are also opened to receive.

You Get What You Pay For

Have you ever parked your car in a no-parking zone, rather than paying to park in a garage or at a meter? Later you find out you have a citation that costs you more than the parking fee would have? I know it's not just me. Sometimes when we try to avoid an ordinary expense, we end up with a consequential cost that's much greater. In business we say you have to spend money to make money. It's the same credence with charitable giving. In order to get money, you have to *give* money.

Death and Taxes

People say there are two things you cannot avoid; death and taxes. If you feel like you can't afford charitable giving because you need every penny of your earnings to survive, I understand.

I have been there.   How do you live off of 80 percent of your income, if you are barely surviving with 100 percent of it?

Start a mindful giving practice by giving away something other than money.   If you don't feel you can give money, give something else.   Give a blanket to a domestic abuse shelter. When you get new slippers for Christmas, give your old ones to a homeless shelter.   Give gently used toys to an orphanage.

The giving will feel so good, you will want to do it more.

ANGELA ELLIS

UNPLUGGING

Unplugging

Research reported by *Disruptive Advertising* suggests that 96 percent of Americans have made at least one online purchase. Furthermore, more than one third of all our shopping is done online rather than in-store. In 2017, online shopping reached $700 billion in sales, which represents a 300 percent increase in just four years. The more we are on our devices, the more likely we are to spend.

Marketers and retailers know this. According to *PR News Wire*, more than 48 million robocalls were placed in 2018. When we're disconnected, we are less susceptible to temptations and scams.

Cell Phones

Depending on how old you are, you might not even remember a time when people only used phones to talk to each other. Now five billion people on the planet are using cell phones for conversation, surfing the internet, making purchases, browsing social media, conducting bank transactions, and sending emails. When I paid off my debt in my twenties, I cancelled my cell phone plan. But in my forties, as a business owner and head of household, that wasn't feasible. Therefore, I'm *not* suggesting you dump your cell phone. Instead, you could talk to your carrier about a plan that might serve your needs at a lower cost. That could mean switching carriers if that will help reduce your bill. Also, consider keeping your current cell phone for two years or more rather than upgrading every time a new version is released.

The coolest kid with the latest gadgets

If you prefer to be the coolest kid on the block with all the latest gadgets, that could be a mindset that is holding you back. Ask yourself if your financial freedom is more important than your ego. I hope it is. And when it's time to get a new phone, sell your old one to a company that buys used phones for cash. Your cell phone company may also offer you a trade-in value for your old phone which can be used toward the purchase of another phone. However, don't *give* your carrier the phone you have already bought and paid for. They will likely refurbish it and re-sell it for their own profit, which doesn't benefit you at all.

Lastly, if your employer requires you to use your personal cell phone for business, request that they foot the bill—at least in part. Talk to your boss about offering you a company-issued device or paying all or some of your cell phone bill. This could reduce your spending by a couple of thousand dollars per year as it did for me.

The Device Trap

My friend Josie has fourteen internet-connected devices in her household of four family members. She, her husband, and her two kids each have a cell phone, a tablet, and a computer. Additionally, they own two video game consoles. That's a lot of data plans and a lot of expense. She says the devices keep the kids occupied. There may even be a false sense of security associated with constant connection. However, with cyberbullying, catfishing, and youth exploitation on the rise, youngsters aren't always safer when they are connected to unknown parties on the worldwide web.

If your little one doesn't have a phone or only has one that calls and texts, they'll be a lot less susceptible to these attacks and you'll be saving money because you won't need as many unlimited data plans. If your kids are teenagers and are a lot more dependent on their devices, consider making their phones their responsibility. I made a deal with my goddaughters. They could keep their cell phones if they were willing to pay for the bill themselves. Also, if they wanted to upgrade to a new phone, they would need to save up for it. Suddenly they drew the conclusion that they didn't need unlimited data plans. They traded in some of their nightly screen time for interactions with each other and quality time with the family.

Social Media

I'll admit when I stopped using social media in 2012 it hurt at first. There was a bit of a weaning off period too. I would leave my cell phone in the car when I went to public places. I would check my social media accounts on my phone when I got back to the car. I discovered that FOMO (Fear of Missing Out) is a real thing. It took about 30 days for me to stop thinking about social media every day. Experts say it takes a month or less, to establish (or break) a habit. Within 90 days, I was not active on any social media. Instead of being constantly plugged in, I would engage in real-time, face-to-face conversations with friends and family. I found that when I'm not using my phone, tablet, or other devices, I'm more connected with real people around me. Trust me, it wasn't always easy. I spent about ten years travelling around the country as I built my consulting business. Travelling alone can be a lonely experience. I spent countless hours in hotels and airports. And, I was often tempted to kill time, boredom, and loneliness with social media and online games. Nevertheless, I had to start exercising some alternatives to protect my finances. Instead of sitting in my hotel room alone, I would take a walk, visit a local museum or park, have dinner at the hotel bar, or take in a movie.

When you are disconnected, it's likely that you will spend less time scrolling through junk mail and watching irrelevant YouTube videos. You might also spend less money when tempting ads pop up. Turn off those notifications that announce the arrival of each incoming communication. This will help you be more selective about what you read, hear, see, and watch. It could also help reduce impulse buying.

Cable TV

When I paid off my debt twenty years ago, I got rid of cable television. I watched movies on DVDs (over and over again) and occasionally treated myself to a two-dollar movie at a local discount theater. Years later, I cancelled cable again and opted for antenna TV and streaming services. As a result, I saved $2,000 each year. Antenna TV is virtually free. There are no recurring costs. I purchased a digital antenna from a local electronics store for twenty dollars. Some of them were priced as high as fifty dollars and boasted a wider range of channels. I was pleasantly surprised to find, there were antenna channels that I didn't even have with cable.

My partner wasn't a big fan of this idea at first. We transitioned away from cable on a trial basis initially. We installed an online streaming service in just one room in our home. We examined our experience with that service after a couple of months. Because we found it to be enjoyable and user-friendly, I was able to convince my partner to switch permanently.

Unplugging can also improve the quality of your life. The Neilson Company reports that adult Americans spend forty-five minutes each day on social media, but eleven hours a day overall on all media. It seems our obsession with knowing what others are doing, how they are living, what they are buying, and where they are going, has reached an all-time high.

When we unplug, we make more time for family, friends, health, and self.

The time you don't spend on media will still be spent. You just have to decide how you will spend it. There is an opportunity here for you to engage more often, and wholeheartedly with those you care about. There is also an opportunity for you to spend more time honing a craft, improving your health, and otherwise taking care of yourself.

IDENTIFYING YOUR HABITS

Identifying Your Habits - Keeping Track

In order to start spending mindfully, you'll need to identify how much you are spending and on what. Until you know what you spend, you won't be able to intentionally cut out wasteful or unnecessary spending in a meaningful way. An extension of the one-month challenge, is this daily practice. Start writing down everything you spend every day. To make this more manageable, consider keeping all receipts. Even when you stop at the gas station and purchase a soda, you'll need to capture that spending. Buying two Cokes a day at the convenience store can really add up in a year's time.

Your major spending categories will include mortgage/rent, food, utilities, phones, insurance, transportation costs, and health care. But chances are, you are spending in lots of other areas as well, like entertainment and clothes. Keep track of all of it. Take a look at your spending in each category. Look for your tendencies to make impulse purchases. Examine non-essential categories where you tend to spend the most. If you are a fashionista, you might be spending the most on clothes. If you are a foodie, dining out could be a large expense for you. Also, take stock of *when* you tend to spend. Is it right after payday? Is it on holidays or special occasions? Is it after a stressful week? This could help you identify some of your emotional triggers. These are occurrences or situations that motivate you to overspend. Emotional spending can keep you in financial bondage. More on this later.

Identify Your Habits - Treating Yourself

Gourmet coffee was my guilty pleasure for years. Every morning, and sometimes in the afternoon, I would treat myself to a flavored hot beverage. What makes it a *guilty* pleasure? I was guilty of spending nearly ten dollars a day on coffee! I did this for years before I wised up. Sure, stopping at a coffee shop for a coffee seems easier than making it at home. Sometimes it is socially gratifying as well. It can be a meeting place and a fun way to connect with others. Nevertheless, I had to ask myself whether it was really worth fifty dollars a week. I started making coffee at home for pennies on the dollar. This one adjustment saved me about $200 each month. I purchased a simple coffee maker from a discount store for twenty bucks. That's a one-time expense that is basically equal to four coffees made by a barista at a gourmet coffee shop.

Chances are, you are eating or drinking away what could be your savings.

Now I can't even recall what my favorite whipped white almond mochaccino tastes like because I haven't partaken in that indulgence in a long time. Maybe your indulgence isn't coffee. Perhaps Sunday brunch, gourmet lunch, cocktails, or gelato sundaes are your preference.

Consider preparing my own dinner at home instead of grabbing takeout on the way home from work. It takes a few extra minutes to make your lunch at home too but could save you $200 to $400 each month.

If you dine out as a family, as a form of entertaining or a time to connect with each other, that's a wonderful thing. Families need quality time, togetherness, and recreation. This could be a weekly or monthly treat, rather than a nightly occurrence. Instead of dinner at a restaurant, consider cooking dinner together at home.

Let good conversation and lots of laughter fill your home and your heart.

You could find this to be a more enriching experience than a restaurant could ever provide. There are certain occasions when you will be dining out with others. My partner and I would meet another couple out for dinner once a week. In an effort to keep my household on track financially, I suggested we have meet for a hike once a week instead. I also recommended that we have dinner at home once a month instead of eating out.

Buying a prepared dinner for four at a local supermarket, was still far less expensive than dinner for four at a restaurant. We eventually eased into a different routine which wasn't always centered around eating. Sometimes we would play card games, take walks around the neighborhood, or play tennis at the park. These activities and other adjustments saved us money while also offering us more variety and fun.

antsegment>

Identify Your Habits - Being Social

One of my girlfriends told me that her weekly wine and dine budget was about a hundred bucks. That's $400 a month! Imagine how quickly she could pay down debt and amass savings with all that consumed cash. She was literally eating herself into financial hardship.

I kept reminding myself of the greater purpose

When I paid off my debt the first time, I was single. As such, it was important to me to get out and socialize with friends on a regular basis. That would often involve costly concerts, festivals, dinners, and excursions. To make the changes I knew I needed to make, I had to stop participating in most of those events. It was radical and difficult and sometimes felt isolating. It was tough to be the odd woman out all the time. Unless it was a very special occasion – like my best friend's birthday – I skipped the concerts, movie nights, comedy shows, and bar crawls.

ANGELA ELLIS

EMOTIONAL BONDAGE

Breaking Even

Kendra gave up her favorite morning latte so she could buy a monthly supply of prestige cosmetics.

Rick gave up cable television so he could buy an expensive sports car.

Joel ended his gym membership so he could use that money toward weekly golf outings.

These clients of mine were not breaking broke with their financial decisions, they were only breaking even. In each scenario they were giving up one thing they really didn't need in order to purchase something else they didn't need. It's the kind of behavior that keeps people broke. When you do this, you gain nothing other than a new item to spend your money on.

People in emotional bondage often allow their circumstances to dictate their behavior.

They think, *"I don't have a large income so there's no way I can save any money."* Or, *"My parents were not well off, so I will never be."* Some even say, *"Debt is just a way of life; there is no way to avoid it."*

Thought processes like these need to change from broke to liberated. A more productive mindset would be: *"I only make ten dollars an hour; therefore, I have to be careful with my spending and diligent about my saving."*

Or, *"My parents were not great financial role models, but that doesn't limit me." Or perhaps, "Debt is a part of my past but won't define my future."*

If you're going to give up cable television, a gym membership, or a daily barista-made beverage, you should use that newly unencumbered cash flow to build something substantial and lasting. Those funds could be invested in a Christmas savings account, a vacation account, or first and foremost an emergency fund.

Size Doesn't Matter

It's against societal norms to take steps that could be seen as social or economic regression. When I got rid of my BMW and purchased a used Honda Accord, my friends and family were shocked. The neighborhood was gossiping. *Could I be bankrupt? Was I struggling financially? I must have been laid off.* What they didn't know is I was making a strategic move. I sold that BMW for $20,000 and bought a used Honda for $10,000. Then I used $1,000 to establish an emergency fund and the remaining $9,000 to pay down some of my debt.

It gave me a nice feeling to ride around in a luxury car and turn heads.

It gave me an even greater feeling to know that I would be debt free in a short while.

I would soon be able to buy what I wanted, travel where I wanted, and do more for my family and community. That was more rewarding than any possession for me.

Am I suggesting you sell your car and buy a less expensive one? Not necessarily. However, if anything you own—house, car, boat, or wardrobe—is bigger and more costly than what you need, downsizing could free up some cash and get you closer to financial freedom. I had a client who would often complain about financial woes. As his career coach, it wasn't my job to solve these issues for him, but I suggested he consider downsizing. It turned out he had a motorcycle that he rarely used. Although he was reluctant to part with it, he was eager to establish some savings and have more disposable income. He sold it by simply posting it on a website and made thousands of dollars.

My friend Dawn discovered clothes in her closet that still had the price tags on them. She had purchased them during a clearance sale at a discount store. She decided to take all those unworn items to a consignment store. She consigned a dozen items and sold them for more than she had paid for them.

Ask yourself what is more important: the boxes of stuff collecting dust in the attic or your family's financial future?

Take a look around your home, garage, backyard, or storage unit for these profitable downsizing opportunities. You could find profits awaiting in and around your house. Again, begin with the end goal in mind.

FREEDOM *IS* FREE

The Simple Things

They say the best things in life are free. During my debt reduction journey, I put this to the test. I knew I didn't want to become a hermit in order to pay off my debts. For me, getting closer to financial freedom meant finding low- or no-cost ways for me to stay entertained. Some of the activities turned into new long-term interests and hobbies. In order to be emotionally and socially healthy and gratified, I needed to remain engaged. I also am a health enthusiast, therefore being active remained a priority.

There are a number of ways I discovered to entertain myself when I was alone. There are also a variety of activities you can enjoy with your friends and family and even the little ones in your life. I've listed a few here. They are all free or cost only a dollar or two. These activities allowed me to save additional money which I applied toward my debts. I call this *Finding Freebies:*

- Take a walk
- Ride a bike (if you have or can borrow one)
- Visit a park
- Play cards and board games
- Build a fire and make S'mores
- Challenge each other to a trivia contest
- Dance in the living room
- Make and decorate cupcakes for each other
- Read books from the library or a thrift store
- Make dinner together
- Talk to each other
- Read magazines and newspapers online (and cancel those subscriptions).

Helping Others

I also found ways to serve the community and simultaneously do some things I enjoyed. There are events everywhere that require the support of volunteers. I've worked registration at art festivals, helped serve at food and beverage events, and been a hostess at silent auctions. I've handed out brochures at music festivals. I've even volunteered to help out at conferences and concerts. In exchange for my time, I get to attend the event for free. I also am able to enjoy the food, beverages, live music, entertainment, and exhibits at the event.

Go online and look for events in your area that need volunteers. Any festival, conference, or fundraiser could possibly need your help. Contact event organizers and ask if they need any volunteers to assist them with the event. There might also be opportunities to volunteer at a mission, soup kitchen, or food bank nearby.

Do It Yourself

According to statista.com, Americans spent more than five billion dollars in beauty salons in 2018. Reportedly, 8.4 billion dollars were spent on nail salon services in the U.S. as well. When I restructured my living and spending, I became my own stylist and manicurist. For those who are deep in debt, like I was, I suggest cutting and styling your own hair and doing your own nails. You could do the same for your children and spouse. My neighbor Chelsey had two small children and didn't have time for hair care. I pointed out to her that spending four hours a month in a salon was not saving her time, and it certainly wasn't saving her money. Also, she admitted that dragging two toddlers to the salon with her was not an easy task. She opted for a low-cost, low-frills style for herself that she could manage easily at home with two toddlers needing her attention.

My family also opted to reduce our dry-cleaning bill by washing and pressing all our clothes. When we did our one-month analysis, we discovered we were spending two hundred dollars every month dry cleaning clothes. Most of those items did not even require dry cleaning! Sure, it was easier to drop the laundry off and have someone else do the work. But we decided to do it all ourselves, because we were not looking for easy; we were looking for savings.

If you have a lawn, doing your own lawn care is a great way to save money as well.

Get outside, get some fresh air, and get the entire family involved.

Pulling weeds and mowing grass can be therapeutic as well. I found myself feeling more relaxed and rejuvenated after spending an hour in the flowerbeds.

I started washing my own car as well—just like I used to when I was in college. I found the old sponges and bucket, rolled up my sleeves, and got to work. Washing my car in my own front yard also afforded me the opportunity to meet a few of my neighbors. You never know who will stop and say hello as they are passing by, walking their dogs, or pushing their baby strollers.

Making meals and coffee at home is also a huge money saver. CNBC reported in 2017 that American households spend more than $3,000 per year dining out. That $3,000 could be spent on debt reduction. Or it could be placed into a savings account.

You and your family could save thousands each year. Once you've completed a one-month spending analysis, opportunities for savings will be revealed. Look at areas where you could be saving in lieu of spending on services you could perform yourself.

TMI - Too Much Information

Whether you want to become a millionaire, save for your children's college, or pay off your debt, you have to understand that there is no magic pill or potion. It will take time and it will take consistent discipline. Be selective with whom you share your plans. The members in your household will need to be aware and, hopefully, they will be on board with your plans.

Everyone in your professional, personal, and social circles won't understand what you're doing to improve your financial state.

Lots of folks will be skeptical because they can't understand the concepts of discipline, sacrifice, and radical change. For most people, freedom from debt is a nice thought, but they consider it to be more of a fantasy than a realistic ideal. Many people simply don't think it's achievable.

When your friends ask you to meet them at the movies or to go to a concert, let them know you're unavailable. Truthfully, you are making yourself unavailable for activities and expenses that don't bring you closer to your financial goals. You don't have to tell them you're working on your finances and reducing your spending. If you do share this, some people would admire or at least appreciate it. Others will not. Either way, you don't owe your associates or even extended family any explanations, justifications, or details. Later on, when you have hoarded enough money to supply your emergency fund, established a savings account, and significantly paid off debts, you might share your success stories to inspire and inform others. Until then, keep a tight lip. If they want to get together, try inviting them to do something *free* with you.

SECOND TIME AROUND

20 years ago, I had successfully paid off $100,000 in debt. It felt good to be completely debt free. I was in a position to help others and I did. I helped some close family members and friends get out of their financial crises. I considered it a blessing to be able to help them because many of them had been supportive of me during tough times in my life.

Then things took another unexpected and costly turn for the worse. I suffered a car accident. My car was completely destroyed, leaving me with no transportation. I was renting a car to get to work every day and that was pretty costly as well. Fortunately, a dear friend loaned me a car. I eventually bought a new automobile, which added tens of thousands in debt to my balance sheet. The insurance coverage was not nearly enough to purchase a new car. I had sustained some injuries during that accident as well. That left me with significant medical bills associated with my chiropractic treatments, physical therapy, and orthopedic care.

Shortly thereafter, there was an additional illness in my household resulting in hospital stays and more medical bills. The debts were really racking up fast. I had about $50,000 in debt at that point and the total was still climbing. Nevertheless, I wasn't worried. I still had money in savings and I still had my emergency fund.

In that same year, the final nail was pounded into the coffin. I lost my job. After seven years with a Fortune 100 company, my entire department was reduced from twelve staff members to three personnel. I was one of the nine who were downsized. At this point I was unemployed and shouldering a host of new debts. Some of those debts I had taken on voluntarily or some I acquired through catastrophe. I was using savings to pay bills and survive. The savings I had amassed over the last several years were quickly depleted. Suddenly, I was $100,000 in debt all over again. This time I didn't have any income to help me out of it.

ANGELA ELLIS

The Recovery Plan

The Budget

I had no regrets about helping my friends and family in their time of need. Of course, I didn't know I would wreck my car, sustain some injuries, and lose my job, all in the same year.

Hindsight is always 20/20.

Nevertheless, my contribution to the security of others was life changing for them and life affirming for me. Although I was frustrated, I wasn't panicked. I knew how to recover, and there was lots of work to be done. I started by creating a budget.

A written budget may seem like a daunting task, but it doesn't have to be. A budget is simply a spending record and spending plan. It helps you analyze your current spending and helps ensure that you have enough money set aside for the things you need. Sticking to a budget can help you avoid debt or make your way out of debt too. To create your budget, make a list of all your areas or categories of spending. This includes but is not limited to food, housing, utilities, automotive, and health care.

A common mistake with budgets is underestimating the depth, breadth, and variety of spending. For example, in your budget, under the automotive category, you will need to include all associated transportation costs, not just your monthly car payment. You will also need to account for gasoline and car insurance. A healthcare budget could include deductibles, prescription drugs, co-payments, over-the-counter medications, insurance premiums, and more. Your budget will have an entry for everything you spend on a recurring basis.

For most of us, there are also expenses that don't occur monthly. They might occur quarterly or biannually. Expenses such as automobiles maintenance, might fall into this category.

To derive your monthly budget for such items, there's a simple formula. Look at what you spend for an entire year and divide it into 12 monthly allotments. I shared this strategy with a former business partner, Lisa, who had spent about $600 that year on maintenance for her car. That included oil changes, brake service, and replacement tires. Lisa had decided to use this strategy to plan ahead for her inevitable car expenses. She divided $600 by twelve to determine her monthly car maintenance costs to be about fifty dollars. Fifty dollars is how much Lisa would need to budget each month to be prepared for these little automotive eventualities when they occur. Lisa used the same process to determine how much to budget for new clothes for her family, birthday gifts for the children, and her summer getaway with her sisters.

Lisa created a budget for her regular monthly spending and then added these items to her budget:

ITEMS	Monthly Budget	Actual Expense
Car repairs	$50	
Summer vacation	$100	
Birthday gifts	$100	
Kids' clothes	$100	
Doctor visits	$50	

If you did the math, you may have noticed that this portion of Lisa's budget totals $400. You may think setting aside $400 a month for unknown expenses is not realistic for you. Let me assure you the cost will occur, and you will have to pay them, whether you or prepared or not. The likely option would be to pay for these things with a credit card or loan. You may not be prepared to start following this plan right now. Instead, this might be a part of your long-term financial recovery plan.

If you use the Breaking Broke techniques, you'll discover money you've been wasting in many areas.

Consistent practices such as *Lean Living, Unplugging, and Downsizing,* will help you free up funds you didn't know were available.

The Emergency Fund

Seventy percent of American households have less than $500 in discretionary funds in the bank or otherwise available to them. Discretionary means this money is not allocated to a bill or other responsibility already. Therefore, you can use it, at your discretion, on non-essential things. Financial experts say that the first kind of savings you should establish is an emergency fund. They recommend having a stash of at least $1,000 dollars set aside for emergencies. I have found that it's best to have an emergency fund which includes $1,000 per household member, but $1,000 total is a good start.

This emergency fund will allow you to pay for unexpected expenses such as illness, injury, job loss, or major home repairs. Depending on your financial situation, you may think you couldn't possibly establish this type of fund. Where there is a will there is a way.

To the naysayer, I issue this assignment: Give yourself a full year and see what progress you make.

If you want to establish a $2,000 emergency fund for you and your spouse, you'll need to start saving $167 each month toward that fund. In a year, you'll have $2,000. Through several *DIY* efforts, a *Cold Turkey Challenge*, and finding free entertainment around town, I stashed away a $2,000 emergency fund in less than five months.

In addition to an emergency fund, I keep an **eventuality fund**. These are occurrences that will happen eventually. Consider these kinds of occurrences that your eventuality funds can help you afford. Does your family take an annual family excursion? Do you have a son or daughter who will be graduating in a year or two? Does your Mom have a milestone birthday celebration coming up? Do you want to attend your cousin's destination wedding? That's what an eventuality fund is for. These aren't the same as emergencies. Emergencies are unexpected (whether you prepared for them financially or not) and require your immediate attention. Not attending to emergencies could have dire consequences. Eventualities are circumstances that you *know* will occur, and in some cases, you know *when* they will occur. If we plan for them, they don't have to cause a financial hardship and they don't have to lead to debt.

I plan for eventualities by budgeting for them. I set a certain amount aside, as a regular line item on my budget, every month for things like this. Every year these eventualities are different, but they always occur, and I'm always prepared.

Shoebox Method

My client's daughter was a sophomore in high school, and she was already talking about studying abroad during her senior year as part of a school exchange program. I advised the client to put a little money away on a weekly or monthly basis for that future event. I advised him to try the **shoebox method**.

The shoebox method helps a person start saving money when they don't have any disposable income available.

At the end of every day my client would empty his loose change out of his pockets and put it into an empty shoebox. Sometimes his loose change would be a couple of quarters. Sometimes his loose change would be a few dollars. Either way, it went into the shoebox. It took about six months for him to put aside a thousand dollars, just by saving his loose change. Of course, there were times when he would deposit five dollars or even a twenty-dollar bill into the shoebox. It took him a few months to realize that if he dropped a little more in, his household wouldn't suffer, he would still be able to pay all his bills on time, and he would get closer to his goal even faster.

If you don't tend to operate on a cash basis, you might use the transfer method instead.   At the end of each day, transfer one or two dollars electronically from your debit card (checking account) to a savings account.   At the end of one year's time you will have saved up to $750 using this method.

Snowball Effect

When I was paying off debts the second time, I used the snowball effect method as well. As a snowball is rolling down a hill it gets bigger and bigger as it goes. As it relates to debt reduction, I paid off my smallest debt first. I put every spare penny I could toward that debt. Then when that was paid off, I started adding that monthly payment to my next smallest debt. That allowed me to pay off my second smallest debt much faster.

Here's how it worked. My largest debt was a credit card. I owed more than $25,000 and I was paying about $200 per month toward that bill. Unfortunately, due to a high interest rate I was hardly making a dent in that balance. It felt endless and hopeless. My smallest debt was a $2,000 medical bill. I diligently used the *Lean Living, Finding Freebies, and Shoebox* methods to help me save up as much money as possible to pay off that $2,000 medical bill within a couple of months.

Once that bill was paid off, I started allocating extra toward my $2,000 appliance bill, my next smallest debt. In addition to the seventy-five-dollar monthly payment I was already making on that appliance bill, I added $150, which is what I had previously been paying toward that medical bill. By paying $225 toward the appliance bill each month, instead of seventy-five dollars, I was able to eliminate it quickly. When that bill was gone, I began paying an extra $225 (previously used on the two bills that I had now wiped out) toward another small debt which was a $1,500 loan. I kept this process going until all the bills were paid in full. It took twenty-eight months! The snowball strategy is a common debt reduction method recommended by financial experts. With diligence and consistency, it's a great technique because it is rewarding. It offers continual gratification, as debts are quickly reduced, and progress is made. This is highly motivating and will encourage you to keep it going.

What To Pay When You Can't Pay It All

My cousin Leo came to me very distraught. He told me he was late on his house *and* car payments. Both were more than sixty days past due. He told me he wasn't sure which one he should pay, but he was certain he could only pay one of the two. He had gotten into this fix for several reasons. He had been hospitalized for a few days and was unable to work during that time as well as during his subsequent recovery period.

Much to his surprise, I suggested he delay paying his mortgage payment and pay his car payment instead. He said, "I'm surprised to hear you suggest that. Most people have told me just the opposite. I have to keep a roof over my head and continue to provide a home for my family."

I recognized that this was a terrible choice to have to make.

If he wasn't already a few months behind on his payments, I would make a completely different recommendation. His credit suffered severely because of the delinquent car and home loans. I made this recommendation to him only because:

1. He was already approaching ninety days late. His credit score had already dropped nearly one hundred points. Making one house payment now wasn't going to change that.

2. He was _not_ going to be able to get caught up on his mortgage within the next ninety days.

I assured him that the security of his family's shelter would not be in jeopardy anytime soon. I explained that while the car company might come and repossess his car, the mortgage company would not come and repossess the house. Therefore, given this tough choice, he should make sure he continued to have transportation to get to work in order to earn money, particularly since he had already been out of work for a few weeks.

Getting to work was essential.

If using mass transit, carpooling, and ridesharing were options for Leo I might have made a different recommendation. However, due to Leo's geographic location, he needed a car. I also recommended he call the mortgage company to inform them of his inability to pay and discuss payment arrangements with them.

Now this isn't an ideal situation. If you did something like this, your credit would take a big hit, and it could become disruptive and uneasy for you and your family if you were faced with this dilemma. This is an unconventional approach to paying past due bills when funds are continually low. And it might not be the best approach for you. Before you make such a choice, there are some things to consider.

Fear of Foreclosure

Yes, homes can be foreclosed. But that's a lengthy process. Typically, lenders send homeowners at least three notices. Then they send pre-foreclosure notices. Then they offer to short sell the house -- sell it for less than it's worth -- which might be the amount due on the loan. If *all* of this fails, then the mortgage company might begin foreclosure proceedings. All the while the homeowner is still living in the home. Of course, the more delinquent you become, the harder it will be to dig out of this debt and the more your credit will suffer. This isn't a decision _not_ to pay your mortgage, this is a realization that you _can't_ pay your mortgage.

Getting Caught Up

Your mortgage is likely to be your biggest household expense. If you let that bill go unpaid, it might be tough for you to recover. Let's say you are three months behind on your mortgage. At $2,000 per month, for example, you would owe the bank $6,000—and counting. It could take years for you to crawl your way out of such a deficit. A smaller expense like a car note or credit card bill might be easier to get back on track even if you've been delinquent for a while. Again, weigh your options and consider short- and long-term implications before making a decision like this. Also, put a recovery plan in place as quickly as possible if any of your bills are past due.

ANGELA ELLIS

FOOLISH CHOICE MINDSETS

Keeping Up With The Joneses

My neighbors were successful and well-employed people. They were both educators living in a middle-class neighborhood, sending their kids to private school, and driving luxury automobiles. Mrs. Culver purchased a new Lexus. Shortly thereafter their friends, the Joneses, bought a new Mercedes. The Culvers wanted so badly to have the best house, newest car, and most lavish lifestyle in their circle of colleagues. They were obsessed with it. Mrs. Culver and her husband agreed to trade in her Lexus and buy a newer, more luxurious car. The Lexus had depreciated in value since she bought it, so she owed much more for it than it was worth. She ended up selling the car back to the dealership for $25,000 while she still owed $36,000 on her car loan. When she bought the new car for $45,000, the dealer added the $9,000 remaining from her Lexus loan to her new car loan. In effect, she was paying $54,000 for her new $45,000 car. I mentioned that the Culvers were lifestyle obsessed. They wanted to be the envy of the neighborhood but, ironically, they were the ones doing most of the envying. Keeping up with the Joneses can be a downfall for any household that makes purchases, seeking notoriety and approval from others.

Heeding Bad Advice

Right after the Culvers purchased their new car, they discovered a hole in the roof of their home. It was causing leaks and water damage inside their house. In order to fix this, they decided to refinance the home. When one refinances, their old loan is replaced with a new one. It's like purchasing the home all over again, just at a different price. That can be an advantageous move, if done at the right time and with the right results.

If you own a home, you could refinance in order to lower your interest rate, lower your monthly payment, or free up some cash. If refinanced for cash, how that cash is used really matters, too. If you plan to get a leaky roof repaired, like the Culvers, you might be making a wise choice. If you're planning to refinance your home so you can buy new wardrobe or a new sound system, you might be making a foolish choice.

The refinance didn't work out favorably for the Culvers because the timing just wasn't beneficial for them. Originally, they had very favorable loan terms: a low, fixed-interest rate. However, when they refinanced, they didn't qualify for the lowest interest rate anymore. At this time, they had a lot of debt which affected their credit worthiness. When they refinanced, they ended up with a high and variable rate. Variable means that at some point during the life of the loan the interest rate could increase. As a result, the monthly payment would increase drastically.

The Culvers were comfortably making their $2,000 monthly mortgage payment, but when the rate changed and they ended up with a $3,000 monthly payment, they were in big trouble. They didn't know how to deal with the situation, and they got some bad advice from some friends. The Culvers decided to continue paying $2,000 each month. They thought the mortgage bank would see this as a good faith effort.

They thought paying something was better than pain nothing

However, the mortgage bank hadn't agreed to this arrangement. Every month that the Culvers paid less than what was due, they were increasingly delinquent on their loan. After a few months of that, the couple received more bad advice. A relative advised them to walk away from their home and cut their losses. That is just what they decided to do. They didn't even put the house up for sale. They simply packed up all their belongings and left the house behind, thinking it would be the bank's problem then. When they moved out, they stopped making payments on that mortgage, even though they still owned the home and it was still their responsibility to pay. Eventually the bank did foreclose, and the Culvers lost everything they had invested in the home for all those years.

Advice is not universal.

Everyone has advice, just like everyone has an opinion. However, not all advice is helpful, nor is it universal. The advice the Culvers received was flawed. It may have worked for the people who advised it, but that didn't make it appropriate for the Culvers and their situation. This book is full of techniques I used to get out of debt, lessons I learned along the way, and even what I learned from the missteps of others. Nevertheless, not every aspect will be appropriate or applicable for everyone.

A Series of Unfortunate Events

My employee, Mike, bought an old, dilapidated truck. He financed it and within a few weeks it was no longer operational. The engine had gone out. The repairs would cost him $850, but he didn't have it. Mike couldn't get to work, so he stopped going. Because he couldn't get to work, he wasn't generating income which affected his ability to pay bills on time. After missing a week of work, he was behind on some of his bills. He knew he needed to keep his job, so he started taking a taxicab to work every day. This was costing him handsomely.

Mike later decided to take a payday loan in order to get the $850 he needed to get his truck fixed. He took out a $1000 loan and pretty soon he had his own transportation again. Unfortunately, the $1000 payday loan required him to pay back a total of $1300, including interest and fees.

Unfortunately for Mike, the truck continued to be unreliable. In less than six months, Mike sunk another $1,000 into repairs on that truck, which was more than the truck was worth.

I talked to Mike about what I thought he could have done differently:

- *It would have been better for him to save up until he could buy a truck that was in better shape.*

- *He could have gone to an auto dealer that offered a warranty or return policy since he ended up with a vehicle that broke down soon after he bought it.*

- *He could have taken the bus to work and avoided the high cost of a taxicab. He would have avoided lost wages as well.*

- *Mike could have stopped spending money to repair the truck, which was ultimately irreparable.*

Mike made a series of errors and paid royally for them.

Following the Foolish

My associate, Al, grew up in a low-income neighborhood in the inner city. He learned some bad habits and received some bad advice from those around him as he was growing up. His uncle, for example, told him never to open a bank account. *"The bank is only trying to steal your money. Keep your money at home,"* he told his nephew. Because he was taught this, Al never opened a savings or checking account. This may sound preposterous, but this is the thinking of many people who haven't had financial role models. It makes perfect sense to them to protect their money this way. They know exactly where it is and have instant and constant access to it, if they keep their money at home.

When Al was hired for a new job, his new employer told him the company only paid via direct deposit. Therefore, he would need a bank account. Al told his boss he preferred to receive a paper check, but his boss assured him that wasn't an option. Al went to a bank, for the first time, at age forty, to open a bank account. Because Al was accustomed to living paycheck to paycheck, he had no money saved up. Therefore, he didn't have the required $200 deposit to open the account. As he searched for a bank with a lower deposit requirement, the weeks rolled by.

The payroll department of his new employer had no way to deliver his wages to him, so he essentially wasn't getting paid. This was extremely frustrating for Al. A coworker told Al that it was illegal for his employer to withhold his pay and suggested that Al file a lawsuit. Al went back to his boss to plead for help and, when that didn't work, he threatened to sue him. Based on the advice of his coworker, Al quit the job and demanded to be paid in full. In keeping with the company's standard procedure, his final paycheck was mailed to him and it took two weeks to arrive. In the meantime, some of Al's bills weren't getting paid and he was incurring subsequent late fees as well.

Following those who don't know and don't have is like "the blind leading the blind."

This is a classic case of following the foolish. Al heeded bad advice of his uncle and coworker. Surely, they were well meaning, but that didn't change the dire situation Al found himself in. Like my employee Mike, Al could have done a few things differently.

- *First, opening a bank account was a must for him. Even if Al had thousands of dollars stuffed under his mattress, he would still not be making the most of his money. In a savings account, his money would earn interest. It would also be safe from theft, flood, or fire.*

- *Al could have asked a relative to lend him the money for the opening deposit.*

- *He could have arranged to have his paychecks deposited into his parents' bank account in lieu of his own. Later, that direct deposit could be changed to his own bank account once he had one established.*

Your closest friends and family aren't always the best sources of good advice. Although they love and care about you, they are not necessarily experts in these matters. Al needed wise counsel from financially prudent friends and family. In the absence of that he should have sought out wise, expert counsel.

Accumulating Stuff

My friend Kendra is a brilliant and talented woman with an auspicious career and a great income. She's also a woman who struggles with financial choices and money management. Every time she gets a sizable pay increase or a promotion, she makes a purchase that is equal to or more than her new earnings. If she gets a new job that pays $10,000 more, she might buy a new car or new furniture. Once, she treated herself to a shopping spree that resulted in an entire new wardrobe: shoes, purses, clothes—the works.

She was learning that the more money she made, the greater the potential for mismanagement and the harder it was to recover from bad decisions. Kendra had been living like this for a year and, as a result, she had no savings, no retirement funds, and no emergency fund. Nevertheless, she owned a lot of cool stuff.

One year, Kendra wanted to take a trip abroad for her birthday. However, she always had trouble putting any money aside for such things. She asked me if she could give me some money every month and requested that I hold on to it for her until it was time for her big trip. It's unfortunate that some people have so little discipline they can't keep their own money, even for a short while. Nevertheless, I agreed to help Kendra.

Every payday, Kendra gave me some money for safekeeping.

Discipline is what allowed her money to grow.

Instead of just holding the money for her, I put it into a money market account and allowed it to earn interest. Over the next few months, Kendra gave me a total of $2,000. At the end of that time, I gave her back $2,200. She was excited about her earnings and asked how it happened. I assured her that discipline is what allowed her money to grow.

Kendra needed to find something that motivated her more than what she could purchase. For someone like Kendra, instant gratification is very tempting. After she saw how her money grew in just a few months, she started thinking about all the money she had blown in the past. She also started thinking about her future.

What do you envision, and what do you want to have in *your* future? What financial choices can you make today that will get you closer to your goals?

IT'S JUST A NUMBER

Challenges with Credit

Asking For Forgiveness

When I decided I couldn't go through life with $100,000+ in debt, I knew some things had to change. I learned from my previous experiences that paying a minimum monthly payment on all my credit card bills wasn't going to put a dent in that debt. I would need to make drastic changes once again. In addition to lifestyle changes, like *Lean Living* and *Finding Freebies*, I decided I needed to ask for forgiveness.

I wrote letters and made calls to all of my creditors requesting a reduction in what I owed them. Most of them were willing to reduce the debt significantly—some reduced it by 40 to 50 percent. When I told a friend about this strategy, she asked, *"Doesn't that take its toll on your credit score?"* My answer was, *"Absolutely. But once you know how to build your credit, a dip in your score is not that alarming."* A credit score is not final, it's always changing, and you can do things to improve it yourself.

The credit bureaus have been asked to release their algorithms for how they determine credit scores. But they won't do it. Why? They are not willing to reveal any tactics that consumers could use to manipulate the system. My guess is they also don't want consumers to figure out how to control their credit or influence their credit rating and their credit report.

You don't need Fair Isaac's algorithms to build your credit. You just need to know what things influence your credit the most so you can build it yourself. It's not some elusive process that's completely out of your hands.

You do have the power.

My creditors were willing to reduce my debts nearly in half. Those charge offs and reductions caused my credit score to drop to 560. Having a large amount of debt along with the debt forgiveness had indeed taken its toll. In less than two years, however, I had moved my credit score from 560 to 720. It eventually soared to over 800.

Accept it and Move Forward

A few years ago, my nephew Peter was newly divorced and jobless. He had been laid off from a job he held for over a decade. During the divorce, he lost the house and the car and was court ordered to pay monthly support for his two children. For several months Peter sulked and lamented over his situation. He stopped socializing with people, started drinking too much, and generally hated his life. I told Peter he had to RAM it.

Recognize it. Accept it. Move forward with it.

Recognize it. Peter took stock of his circumstances. He was $50,000 in debt. He owed his ex-wife $1,000 in monthly child support. Unfortunately, he was making less money than he needed to live. Peter's credit score was 580. Lastly, some of his bills were sixty days past due as well.

Accept It. Even though things seemed bleak, Peter needed to accept his situation. He needed to acknowledge it as real, but *not* as permanent. He knew he wanted to change it and there was only one more thing to do.

Move forward with it. Peter began the journey to rebuild his credit. I helped him better understand his credit score and what impacts it. Here are a few of them:

Debt to income ratio: how much money you make compared to how much money you owe.

To figure out yours, divide your monthly <u>debt</u> payments by your monthly <u>gross</u> income. The ratio is expressed as a percentage, and lenders use it to determine if you can afford to repay a loan. For example, if you earn $4,000 per month and you owe $2,000 each month, your debt to income ratio is 50 percent. Peter's was a whopping 80 percent. 25–30 percent is considered desirable.

Available lines of credit: how much money you have available to you from creditors.

Peter had four credit cards. Those credit cards offered him $20,000 in available credit. When creditors are willing to trust you with a higher credit line, it's important to keep the balance owed low. You do that by charging very little and/or paying off loans quickly. This will drive your credit score up.

Delinquent accounts: when you miss a payment or pay late.

The number of delinquent accounts you have and how far behind you are on paying those loans is part of how creditors evaluate your creditworthiness. Peter had three delinquent accounts. Once he got those accounts all caught up, his credit score increased by thirty points.

Living on $30,000 a year was a real struggle for Peter as well. Prior to being laid off, he was making three times that amount. Peter decided to start a lawn care service to earn more money. He had his teenage sons help him with the work and was able to earn an additional $3,000 per month. With this new income, he paid off all of his credit cards in full. Not only did this reduce his debt to income ratio, it improved his credit score by another forty points.

Peter called his creditors and asked them to change the due dates on some of his bills. Instead of paying all his bills on the first of the month, he staggered those payments, making all his bills due at different times of the month. This made it easier for Peter to pay all his bills on time.

No Credit Equals Bad Credit

My cousin Rebecca had no credit at all. She bought everything with cash, which is great. She was determined not to be in debt, so she avoided loans. At some point in life, Rebecca wanted to buy a house. She knew she would need to apply for a mortgage.

In some situations, no credit can pose the same challenges as bad credit. Rebecca's credit had to be built before she could qualify for any type of home loan. She even had trouble renting an apartment without any established credit. I suggested Rebecca apply for a secured credit card.

To get a secured card, she deposited $200 into an account established by the credit card company. She could then use the card the company provided to her to make charges. She was basically using her own money to make charges, up to $200. She charged the entire $200; and as soon as her secured card bill arrived, she paid the balance in full. Even though she was using her own money, she was also showing her ability to pay.

Then she got another secured card. This credit card company was willing to give her twice the amount of her deposit. She deposited $250 to secure the card, and the company gave her a credit line of $500. Every month she would charge a few hundred dollars and pay it off as quickly as possible. When those card companies reported her payment history to the credit bureaus, her credit score drastically increased.

Freeze Your Accounts

Once you pay off a credit card bill, you may be tempted to close the account. Don't do it. Closing a credit card account will impact your credit in a way that's unnecessary and not helpful. Instead, just stop using the cards. Stop carrying them in your wallet. Cut them up.

My partner suffered from separation anxiety. He would literally experience anxiety when separated from his charge cards. So, I froze his accounts for him. I put all his credit cards into a plastic bowl, filled the bowl with water, and put it in the freezer. He still had his credit cards and the accounts were still open; he merely wasn't able to easily access them. It may seem extreme or even silly, but it proved to be an effective way to stop unwanted impulse purchases. If my partner wanted to purchase something, he would have to wait until his card thawed out. Hopefully, by then, the urge would pass.

FINAL LESSONS

Lazy is as Lazy Does

Laziness has great endurance. What is in motion tends to stay in motion. What is stationary tends to remain stationary. This law of physics applies to people too.

My friend Kasey quit her job and announced she was retiring early. That's great, right? A cause for celebration! The problem was she hadn't prepared for retirement in any way. She took in roommates to bring in income, but her roommates caused lots of additional expenses for her. Within a year her house needed significant repairs, including a new HVAC system, some plumbing work, and a new refrigerator. Her utility costs were skyrocketing as well. Kasey simply failed to prepare for early retirement but was trying to force it to work without preparation. She eventually took a part-time job to make ends meet.

The most challenging part of this process will be getting started. But once you start, you will keep moving. That movement will include changes in behavior, changes in perspective, seeking out knowledge, and aligning with new mentors.

If you decide you're not going to work at improving your finances, you will reap the benefits of that decision.

That may mean disappointment, poverty, anxiety, and worse. If you don't do much, you can't expect much in return. Sometimes a person's lack of financial responsibility has evolved over time. Traits like this can be passed down from generation to generation.

Perhaps you've been conditioned to mismanage your money. You may not even recognize where these tendencies originated. Nevertheless, you can—with some degree of effort—change that trajectory. Even though you've developed certain habits over the years, you have the opportunity to change them and have an impact on your life and the next generation.

Be Convinced

When I started my debt, reduction plan the first time, I was single. When I told married friends, family, and clients about my financial strategies and my debt elimination journey, they said to me, *"That's easy for you because you're single."* I've explained to those skeptics that no process of paying off six-figure debt should be described as "easy."

It takes diligence, sacrifice, consistency, and sometimes creativity.

Frankly, I see it as an excuse or a way out. If you can convince yourself that your situation is different than mine and therefore insurmountable, then you can convince yourself not to try. And if you never try, you never have to take the risk of failing.

Years after my initial debt payoff, I helped my significant other use these same methods to pay off back taxes, eliminate credit card debt, and buy his first home. Later I was able to help my grown stepchildren work through their financial woes using some of these techniques.

If you are convinced you are stuck where you are, then there you are.

Based on that belief you will make choices and life decisions that keep you in that condition. But if you are convinced that you can have more, do better, make a difference, and make a change, you will ultimately achieve just what you think you can achieve.

Be convinced that you're worthy.

In my journey to financial freedom I've talked to hundreds of people who don't believe they are capable of a better life. A great author once said, *"We are not great, because we fear our own greatness."* Don't be your own obstacle. Get out of your way.

ANGELA ELLIS

Getting Started

Getting Started

Newton's third law says that for every action there is an equal and opposite reaction. Even when I dug my way out of debt once, I still ended up deep in debt a second time. Sometimes I experienced financial hardship because I made poor decisions. Other times I experienced hardships because of life circumstances that I caught me off guard. Either way, I had to make a commitment to a new mindset, new behaviors, and a new process to turn the hardship into a success story.

You must be intentional about climbing your way out of the hole that life has dug for you. Even if you don't succeed at first, you'll learn from it and try again. Failure is not final unless you stop trying.

It has been a humbling experience to realize I don't have all the answers. You don't have to have all the answers either, and you don't have to be perfect. You just have to get started.

Each step counts as long as they are steps in the right direction.

If you walk twenty steps in the right direction, you will be twenty steps closer to your destination. Devise a plan now. Start by identifying where you want to go. Then you can figure out how to get there.

Action Plan

What do you want to achieve in your life?

What do you want to achieve financially?

By when do you want to achieve this financial goal?

Which one of the broke mindsets has been holding you back?

Impressions   keeping up with Joneses   laziness

following the foolish   impatience

When will you complete a written budget?

_____/_____/20__

Which Breaking Broke methods will you use to get started?

shoebox   snowball   debt-forgiveness

downsizing   30-day cold turkey

30-day spending analysis

Which techniques will you recommend for your family or leverage for yourself?

living lean   finding freebies

do- it -yourself   reduce device traps

Budget Form

Category items	Projected Spending	Actual Spending
HOME		
Mortgage		
Utilities		
CAR		
Insurance		
Car note		
Gas		
HEALTH		
Prescriptions		
Insurance		
OTC meds		

Contact lenses		

FOOD		
Groceries		
Dining out		
CHARITIES		
Church		
Salvation Army		
School fundraisers		
HOME GOODS		
Toiletries		
Cleaning products		
PET CARE		
Food		

Meds		
BEAUTY		
Cosmetics		
Haircuts		
CLOTHES		
T-shirts, undies, and socks		
School uniforms		
Work clothes		

Glossary of Terms

Emergency Fund

A savings of $1,000 per household member set aside for unexpected, urgent, and necessary expenses, such as injuries/healthcare, car repair, or home damage.

Eventuality Fund

A savings of a predetermined amount for occurrences – like an out-of-town graduation that you know are happening in the next year.

Shoebox Method

Put money, specifically your extra or loose change, into a shoebox every day as a way of accumulating savings.

Transfer Method

Electronically transfer one dollar a day from a checking/debit account to a savings account.

Keeping Track

Writing down every amount spent for one month, followed up by analyzing expenditures that could be eliminated.

Budget

A record of what you spend and what you intend to spend in your household each month.

80-10-10 Rule
Use 80 percent of your net (take home) income to live, contribute 10 percent of said income savings of some kind, and dedicate 10 percent to charitable giving.

Living Lean
Reduce spending by eliminating unnecessary expenditures from one's lifestyle.

Device Trap
Having too many electronic devices which bring extra expense to one's household.

Safe Keeping
Giving someone money, temporarily, to prevent oneself from spending it.

Snowball Effect
Pay your smallest loan or debt off first. Apply what was the monthly payment for the smallest bill to the next smallest bill you have. Continue paying off debts and applying larger

monthly payment to each revolving bill you have—until all debts are paid in full.

Finding Freebies
Entertain yourself and your family by finding free forms of exercise, entertainment, and recreation.

Secured Credit Card
A charge card that is secured with your own money placed into an account. When charges are made using that card, the cardholder is using their own money.

Debt to Income Ratio
How much money you make compared to how much money you owe. Derive by dividing monthly debt payments by monthly gross income. The ratio is expressed as a percentage.

Waiting It Out
A process of delayed gratification which involves waiting until to buy an item when you can buy it with cash.

Cold Turkey Challenge
Refrain from making any purchases for one month. Pay your bills and attend to physiological needs (food, shelter, healthcare, safety). Buy nothing else.

Financing Your Fun

Planning and saving for fun things like vacations and new electronics. This could include having a garage sell, getting a second income, or selling your own goods and services. For this month, and the preceding month, purchase groceries as you normally would, refill your prescriptions as needed, and pay your bills on time.

Angela Ellis is owner and Chief Learning Officer of Enhance Business

Solutions, LLC. Angela's expertise as a coach and learning facilitator stems from twenty years in Human Resources and Organizational Development. She provides clients with leadership effectiveness tools, performance improvement strategies, and team synergy ideas through individual coaching, group coaching, and classroom learning engagements. Her international client base includes government entities, Fortune 500 companies, universities, and more.

She is an International Coaching Community certified coach. She also holds several other certifications in her field.

She is a 2020 Athena Award nominee which recognizes women for their service, mentorship, and leadership. She is also a recipient of the *Forty Under 40* Award and the Nashville Emerging Leader Award (NELA).

She is a philanthropist and a community advocate with a passion for serving women, children, and elders. Additionally, she serves on various nonprofit boards.

Angela is originally from Baton Rouge, Louisiana.

Made in the USA
Columbia, SC
30 September 2020